Copyright © 2018 Tekkan
Artwork Copyright © 2018

All rights reserved.
First Printing, 2018
ISBN 978-1-7324107-6-3

To contact Tekkan please email:
buddhaboy1289@gmail.com

Table of Contents

Waiting and Loving . . . . Page 91

How to Read My Poems

I have married the sonnet to the tanka. I tell a story in the sonnet — using three quatrains, separated by line spaces, and a final couplet. The story builds to a conclusion in the couplet. The tanka is a commentary, or a counterpoint, to the sonnet — the combined poems have two endings.

I don't rhyme my sonnets, because I want freer expression. I want to be direct in my meaning — I want people to clearly understand my meaning. The metaphors are inspired by Shakespeare, and the (aimed-for) precision is in imitation of Japanese style. Using the sonnet with the tanka, I am mixing the sensibility of the Occident and the Orient — which I have done by living in England, Japan, and America.

I don't punctuate much in my poetry. I want the words themselves to do the work. There is logic between words, and the forms provide structure. By not using punctuation I hope to direct readers to carefully attend to each word — to appreciate the graininess of words.

Reading my poems silently, say, on a bus, a train, or an airplane, and reading them aloud, may be different experiences. The way I've written there's not always a pause intended at the end of the line. Hint: *My poems are to be recited not as lines, but as phrases, and a phrase often overflows the break at the end of a line. I pause and take a breath where it seems natural for me to pause. Another person may pause differently than I do.*

Each single poem is a piece of a mosaic, and it is my hope that the collection of poems form an accurate portrait of consciousness.

My daughter, Jocelyn MacDonald, is a wonderful artist. Her art work graces this book.

I am Barry MacDonald. I received the *dharma* name, *Tekkan*, which means, Iron Man, a settled practitioner of great determination.

— *Tekkan*

Everyday Mind VII

Snow is melting and
water is flowing
downhill across the
streets of Stillwater
and joining the river.

This is the time of the husk of winter
When snow is melting in the afternoon
And freezing again overnight so that
There are puddles on my driveway that I

Step around to keep from getting my shoes
And socks wet during the day and yet I
Could slip and fall on the early morning
Ice — and as I'm driving about town there

Are piles of towering snow bordering
The parking lots of Stillwater that are
Gradually disintegrating and
Every year I mark the progress of their

Disappearance as the arrival of
Spring while sunlight is generating strength.

Downhill from my house
on the south side of
the street under a
shady pine every
year the last snow melts.

The dawning light through the stained glass windows
Filling space inside the capacious church
Sanctuary is different from that
Of two weeks ago as the sparkle of

The blues reds greens and golds of the glass is
Prominent and the pews and organ are
More visible and the candle light that's
Hanging on a chain from a wooden beam

And enclosed in a red glass container
Is no longer aglow in the darkness
But it still inspires a glow of warmth
Inside me as each of us is stepping

Quietly in line and meditating
With every step around the empty pews.

There is more light
in March but the air
is chilly and I look
forward to walking
barefoot in July.

After the Big Bang when the universe
Exploded from the size of a pinpoint
And thereby created the substance of
Space/time for millions of years clouds of gas

Radiated outwards that the force of
Gravity collapsed into the first stars
And for billions of years in the cores of
The most massive of stars where the pressure

Of gravity and temperature is
Highest nuclei of atoms were fused
Together forming new elements like
Oxygen and carbon and iron and

When the original stars convulsed and
Irrupted the cosmos was evolving.

The iron and carbon
in my body came from
a supernova billions
of years ago but how
did consciousness arise?

The laws of science can explain light and
Gravity and nuclear behavior
And by using radio-telescopes
Scientists can travel back in time and

Observe the radiation left over
From the Big Bang at the remotest edge
Of the cosmos in any direction
And they postulate that the universe

Is expanding — and they have fashioned their
Minds into marvelous instruments but
They have no explanation for how their
Consciousness came to be except to say

The random interaction of matter
Somehow produced their curiosity.

Perhaps the cosmos
is permeated
with consciousness and
the galaxies and the
atoms are its body.

A watery snow in April summons
The worst in me because I clear my own
And my mother's driveway too every time
The weather turns and in April I think

It shouldn't be snowing anymore and
It should be raining — if there is any
Disharmony within my acquaintance
It is sure to blossom in resentment

As I am moving snow — but I know my
Emotions are wayward and I practice
Letting them go and when I am finished
Writing this poem my mood will be light —

April snow is not the worst occurrence
And I am grateful I can change my mind.

Two hurricanes in
Puerto Rico
devastated the island
leaving everyone bereft
and sweltering in summer.

I am looking at a blue sky through a
Window sitting on a comfy office
Chair with arm rests warm and comfortable
In early April when there shouldn't be

Any snow on the ground after I raked
Snow from one roof and cleared two driveways and
Two walkways and one porch with my fingers
On the edge of freezing and now I am

Drinking coffee and the snow is piled as
High as it was months ago and is the
Quantity of light greater than it was
But the season is overwhelmed by an

Intrusion of arctic air or is the
Earth wobbling and bringing an ice age?

I dreamed of driving to
Baraboo Wisconsin in March
to converse with a
friend but this morning it seems
February has returned.

It is anomalous for April to
Be as frozen as February in
The morning and it seems that the jet stream
In the troposphere is flowing in a

Pattern and sweeping Minnesota with
Arctic snow and cold when in other years
We would be seeing tulips by now and
This morning while driving down a hill I

Saw several kids huddled in a group
Waiting for a school bus as a gust of
Wind raised some freshly fallen snow from a
Pile by the street and the snow swirled in

The air and I saw one little girl's long
Hair streaming in the wind for a moment.

I lose my morning
clarity moving
snow before it melts
and clogs the blower
in the afternoon.

There is a robin in the apple tree
And another has appeared and they are
Hopping about the tree and on the ground
And now they are gone and everything else

Outside my window doesn't look like spring
And I am grateful we didn't get the
Four to eight inches of snow forecasted
And we only have a frosting of snow

This morning but I am losing track of
Time and where did the months go while I was
Looking out this window looking forward
To spring and yet the same bare brown branches

Are stretching under a white sky and the
Sun is a white disk with a white halo.

My authority
the weather app on my phone
shows temperatures
in the forties and fifties
on Tuesday Wednesday and Thursday.

The nearest star to earth is four million
Light years away and yet there are billions
Of stars whirling around the massive black
Hole at the center of our galaxy —

The Milky Way — and our sun and earth and
Our neighboring planets are orbiting
Together in a spiral around the
Black hole at two hundred kilometers

Per second and yet it takes two hundred
Forty million years for us to orbit
The galaxy — and the galaxy as
A whole is careening at six hundred

Kilometers per second within a
Cluster of interwoven galaxies.

We are like clever ants
with glasses who are
scrutinizing and
conceptualizing
dark mass and energy.

I admire the romance of the stars
Leonardo Dicaprio and Kate
Wislet in the iconic scene of the
Movie *Titanic* at the prow of the

Ocean liner when they face the icy
Wind and ride the turbulence of the sea
And I would like to do the same but I
Don't know which direction to stand into the

Rotation of the earth on its axis —
And I would like to ride the turbulence
Of space as the earth is going about
The sun — and join the solar system

Sojourning around the galaxy — but then
Where on earth is the galaxy going?

Gripping the armrests
of a comfy chair I am
tumbling in four
directions at once without
a smidgeon of dizziness.

It is fun to play with the lingo but
When talking to a real scientist I
Get a little dizzy and I am not
Sure whether my question is bizarre and

Is he saying something intelligent
That seems to make sense or is he confused
And doesn't know the answer or is he
Passing on some knowledge and in effect

Is saying — you figure it out — because
I really want to know the direction
From where I am now to face into the
Rotation of the earth on its axis

But all he did was point to the sun and
Remark that is where to get my bearings.

I wonder whether
disorientation and
dizziness has a
relation to the wavy
wacky multiversity.

Today is the seventy-forth day of
February with snow in the forecast
For tomorrow and in two days also
With an intervening day of sun to

Imagine what spring would be like if it
Came and now I am resting after the
Snow blower sputtered and expired and I
Shoveled a foot of heavy snow with the

Snow sticking to the shovel and I knocked
The shovel on its side on the asphalt
To un-stick the snow from the metal and
Then I thrust and knocked and thrust and knocked and

Finally I am finagling like
Crazy to turn complaints into humor.

The earth revolves and
the sun is stationary
so when I see the rising
sun I am facing the
earth's rotation.

On this the seventy-fifth — and the first
Of its kind — day of February I
Established for myself a separate
Peace and because my snow blower is broke

I will do as the people of yore have
Done after another fall of snow and
I am determined now to tred upon
The snow and crush it and not remove it

By shovel or other mechanical
Contrivance and I shall not think about
The snow or be disturbed about the snow
But yea will I remember that the Lord

Gaveth and the Lord will taketh away
And the sun will shine and the day be good.

Nicolaus Copernicus
was the first to see
the sun is not rising
the earth is spinning
towards the morning sun.

There may be a heaping of snow on the
Ground in the second half of April and
The trees are frozen in time just as they
Were in December and the chill rising

From the piles of snow is penetrating
But the robins have returned and today
I saw a squadron of the tiniest
Ants trespassing on the kitchen floor — and

The sun is half way up in the morning
And is a glorious force coming through
The window — and crystals in the snow on
A bush a foot away from me through the

Glass are refracting the sunlight into
Pinpoint jewels of green blue red and yellow.

So many things are
transpiring at once
coming and going and
even my emotions
even out.

We haven't seen Karl for a long time and
We don't know when the meeting ends whether
We will see each other again but if
There's a history of attendance it's

Easy to assume we will meet again
Tomorrow — not everyone comes every
Morning but some of us come several
Times a week so we rely on a room

Full of drunks wanting sobriety and
Assuming a sense of mission who are
Working a program of recovery
And we are more light-hearted together

And we speak honestly among ourselves
Which is much better than drinking alone.

Over time some of
us return crestfallen
after a bout of
drinking to a welcome
but some of us disappear.

Even when April rain is replaced with
Snow there is radiance in the season
When a crust of leftover ice is on
The ground and a bitter wind is howling

Through the days and the sky is mostly grey
There is radiance as we celebrate
Karl who died of alcoholism and
Grief because his son died before him and

We are gathered in the sanctuary
In the middle of an April blizzard
Remembering Karl's buoyancy and his
Big hearted bantering and the light is

Mingling with the clouds and the snow and
Becoming radiant in the stained glass.

The radiance is
mixed with sorrow and
we shouldn't be hard
on ourselves for
questioning.

A solar wind radiates outwards from
Our sun far surpassing the planets of
Our solar system making a bubble
That scientists call a heliosphere

Where pushing out encounters pushing back
From interstellar space and because the
Sun rotates once every twenty-five days
There is a spiraling of magnetic

Wind particles flowing out to meet a
Continuously shifting boundary
Where the solar wind slows and stops — where the
Pressure of the interstellar wind is

Enough to create a balancing of
Whirlwinds permeating the universe.

In Minnesota
a jet stream of polar air
is turning spring rain
into winter blizzards and
all I can do is wait.

The sparrows in the apple tree are here
For an instant and are going while the
Air is moist and the sky is threatening
To snow — and I am frustrated waiting

For a friend to do what needs doing and
Am wondering if I could have managed
Better — and I would like to give as much
Weight to my frustration as I do to

The sparrows in the apple tree and I
Would like to pretend the gloomy day is
No more imposing than a summer cloud
But things are happening just as they are —

I will improvise and do what I can
And tomorrow will be another day.

Sparrows are flitting
an eagle is circling
a squirrel is hopping
in the soggy snow and
I am watching.

It may be below freezing now and cold
Enough to snow — and the two driveways I'm
In charge of may be half covered from the
Last falling of snow — because my blower

Broke and I was too disgusted with the
Snow trespassing too far into April
To make the effort to shovel the whole
Driveway — but the forecast temperature

For this afternoon and the next four days
Is above freezing and is for mostly
Clear skies and so I can savor the chill
Rising from the snow as the weakening

Embrace of winter and I will wash my
Polar fleeces and put away my boots.

All the bare branches
of these drab brown trees
will be sprouting buds
and then the leaves will
be sighing in the breeze.

Henry has kidney disease and there is
No cure but symptoms are treatable with
A syrupy concoction that I draw
Into a syringe in the morning and

The evening and he sees me coming
But I am quicker and I get behind
Him and pull his face back and quick like the
Devil the medicine squirts down his throat

That he doesn't like so much but soon gets
Over when I give him his food — I do
All this while groggy from waking up and
As the minutes go by I enjoy my

Alertness and when I clean the box I
Notice his urine is syrupy goo.

It is sticky
going in and sticky
coming out and
the cat box is
messy.

Kit lets me know when he wants more food by
Knocking a container off the kitchen
Counter onto the floor and then he looks
At me and yowls and I see he's got me

Trained as I could choose not to respond but
Usually he gets as much as he
Wants because he insists and I'd rather
Have quiet in the house — but every day

I notice there are new scabs about the
Top of his head and inside and outside
Of his ears and I wonder whether he
Itches all the time or he is nervous

And is compelled to punish himself by
Scratching furiously with his hind nails.

In the world of
cat psychology
do maladjustment
and phobia arise
with intelligence?

It is easy to do the same thing at
The usual time to balance chaos
And when I am spooning cat food into
Dishes and separating the three cats

So that they don't trespass on each other
I could be burning with frustration with
A person who is not present at the
Moment or when I am brushing each cat

And also singing to them I may be
Occupied with a little triumph of
Yesterday but if I am nimble in
The morning especially nimble I

May be able to simply spoon the cat
Food and then brush each of the cats in turn.

Instead of falling
into a funnel of
emotion I would
rather sing nonsense
to the cats.

Time is slow after forty minutes of
Meditation in the morning because
The sitting quietly is like leaving
The aperture of a camera open

Enough to accumulate light and more
Of the world enters my gaze — and it takes
A long time for a bird to cross from one
Tree to another — and I admit

How tricky it is to identify
The beneficial effects of doing
Zen — because I will never know how I
Would have behaved apart from doing Zen

But I believe I am more thoughtful which
Is something I could easily have missed.

Years of meditation
allows more of life
to accumulate.

It is not every day that the sky is
Open but when it is I can see the
Contrails of airplanes in the distance — and
The warmth descending today creating

Puddles everywhere is a welcome change
And the bush outside the window is free
Of snow and sparrows are hopping up the
Trunk of the cottonwood and little birds

Are flitting between the trees in the back
Yard and there isn't any wind and I
Watch everyday but rarely see that the
Atmosphere and sunlight make a blue sky

On a clear day with a white rim along
The far horizon and I don't know why.

Last week a dozen
eagles were circling
slowly not far up
and sparrows were
darting below them.

On a third day of a clear sky I am
Driving between Stillwater and Bayport
And there are the crumpled leaves from autumn
And the morning sun is drenching the grass

And the grass is beginning to green and
I see the bare branches of bushes and
Trees that at a distance look like smudges
But in passing their twiggy forms emerge

Into wild curves and crooks and every limb
And twig is reaching up and outward to
Capture rays of sun and I remember
How winter wind sounds in barren branches

And what a difference the leaves will make —
The difference of howling and sighing.

Even when I am
driving by and occupied
with politics the
trees communicate
messages.

The comprehensive effects of winter
Are easy to miss month after month as
I hunker down and limit myself but
With the lifting of the temperature

There is liberation and today I
Rummaged through a container of shoes and
Discovered shoes untouched and forgotten
For a dozen years and I am appalled at

Some of the judgments I made and am
Sorry for the money wasted but am
Also enthused to put on a spiffy
Style in spring because it's been depressing

To wear the boots spattered with the salt the
Road crews use to melt the ice on the roads.

Like a turtle
in a shell I
sheltered within
but spring summons
peacock flamboyance.

I was given the lens of seeing and
The ear of hearing coming along with
The responsibility of choosing
And creating a direction that suits

Me that no one else can duplicate — and
When I am ruminating and searching
For words I sometimes do touch a meaning
That is difficult to communicate

And it is important to cultivate
The conviction that the messages I
Am seeing hearing intuiting are
The messages I am meant to receive

Because I am an individual
Swimming in a sea of interaction.

Experience is
transforming
with every step —
outside in and
inside out.

Is there any escaping the tension
Between love and hate even if there is
Awareness that whatever I perceive
Is only a slice of a larger whole

And even if there is exhaustion with
Competition and belligerency
Is it possible by an exercise
Of will to extinguish the revulsion

But preserve that which captivates my heart
Because emotions arise within me
And sometimes I chose the arising and
Sometimes the arising chooses me and

Anyway my consciousness is consumed
With reverberating contradictions.

Teachers convey
compassion
benevolence
equanimity and
altruistic joy.

It is necessary to see anger
Is the problem and it doesn't matter
Whether it is justifiable and
Doesn't matter if it's motivating

Anger alters reality and is
Difficult to escape — and it fills a
Body with furious energy but
Afterwards there is deflation and self-

Pity — and anger radiating out
Invites recrimination coming back
Without remedy — but imagine joy
And happiness and liberation and

What could be more vital than evading
Cancerous inexhaustible anger?

The world is burning
from a point of view
but today the sun
is brilliant and the
sky is resplendent.

There is a cosmos beyond the blue sky
That humanity has been ignorant
Of until quite recently and we are
Lucky to have a single sun and a

Moon that balances the earth's wobble that
Provides us with reliable seasons
Because it's not uncommon for two or
Three suns to orbit each other making

Stability impossible for a
Planet and imagine being on a
Planet flung into interstellar space
By the wild oscillations of two suns

Because without a sun at just the right
Distance we would not have a shining sky.

The sun the moon and
sky are mysterious
and miraculous but
usually we are too
busy too notice.

Gravity collapses clouds of gas to
Create the stars of differing sizes
And many are more massive than our sun
But the mass of every one is crushing

Inward on a core where the pressure on
The nuclei of atoms overcomes
The resistance of positive charges
To fuse the protons together and an

Explosion of energy and heat and
Light pushes outward and establishes
An equilibrium of forces and
From the core of our sun it will take ten

Million years for a photon to reach the
Surface — and eight minutes to strike the earth.

Energy passes
through my optical lens and
through my synapses
to my visual cortex
and then I can see the clouds.

There are nights when I am lying in bed
And cannot turn off my thinking and thoughts
Go around and around signifying
Nothing but restlessness and there are nights

When I am a hero in epical
Fantasies and once I was flying in a
Stadium and everyone was watching
Me but it's necessary every day

To provide myself with a good night of
Sleep and even if I become wide-eyed
With fear in a phantasmagorical
Dream I need the separation from the

Normal tensions and frustrations of life
Because when I sleep well I am awake.

Sometimes I wake up
wrapped in the sheets like
an eggroll because
my body begat
centrifugal force.

There is no mitigation of the shame
And no deflection of the anger that
The drunk who drives and injures innocent
People incurs especially when he

Understands the next drink could trigger a
Loss of consciousness when in the act of
Walking and talking and drinking he no
Longer knows what he is doing — except

To say that the alcoholic can't stop —
And the condemnation of the world will
Not change the fact until he surrenders
And time in jail or in prison may be

Justified and helpful in creating
A moment of healing desperation.

Alcoholism
progresses like
Alzheimer's and the
personality
slowly goes.

Little green buds are dotting the trees of
Stillwater and the sun — half way up — is
A brilliant disk radiating warmth and
The green of the grass is assertive and

Unstoppable and days of snow and ice
Of snow falling from a white sky with an
Absent sun and penetrating cold with
Piles of snow lining the streets everywhere

Those days are impossible now and yet
I am weary from the lingering fact
Of winter and when I see a friend with
The clarity of spring there are wrinkles

Around his eyes I didn't see before
Lending a smile a little more meaning.

I saw a pair of
cardinals one after the
other frolic in
the bush outside the window
before they flew away.

It is a day I've been expecting for
Many days and I would have to be dead
Not to celebrate the awakening
Of spring because my body has endured

Another winter and I remember —
And there is a bizarre simplicity
That a disk of white fire rising in an
Empty sky could prompt the budding trees and

The growing grass — and the curving twigs of
The cottonwood are sporting sprays of seeds
That look like decorations and when I
Close my eyes my eyelids are red with light

And my face is bathed in warmth again and
I imagine myself a tomato.

A cardinal flies
from a lower to a
higher cottonwood branch
and the sun makes
its wings shine.

Once I got on an airplane and went to
The other side of the earth to find home
But when arriving I was a stranger
To myself and to the Japanese — who

Didn't ask me to come — I wanted an
Adventure and excitement and I learned
Excitement is the management of a
High level of fear — and for the nine years

Of living in Japan I encountered
Unpredictability and turning
Points and when returning to Stillwater
I discovered more unpredictable

Turning points and where ever I reside
There is something unexpected coming.

We are human animals
growing roots into the
stories we tell ourselves
in an effort to manage
unpredictability.

I am awash in waves this morning with
The windows of my car open with the
Warmth coming in and I am bombarded
With the vibrant blue and white of the sky

And I am absorbing an explosion
Of tiny green leaves on the browns of the
Trees and an exhibitionist in a
Purple shirt is walking with his dog and

There is a sprinkling of dandelions
Already and a red wing blackbird is
Flying and when I get to the office
To play with words a yellow and a red

Tulip by the garage are reminding
Me cresting waves of light are everywhere.

Waves of light rippling
in the air enveloping
me separating me
from winter are exactly
what I wanted.

We were talking about how to deal with
Alcoholics from a family point
Of view and the two older ladies who
I assume came together as comrades

Were listening attentively next to each
Other with upside down smiles and they were
Calm and serious and settled within
Themselves and it was apparent they were

Capable of separating nonsense
And propriety and while bringing a
Message of spirituality and
Hope I find humor is harmonious

With the mission and I thought I saw a
Twinkle in their eyes of acknowledgement.

While sharing a
message of recovery
there is resonance
with the words in the
slightest of gestures.

I left my phone charging all night again
And it was very hot when I unplugged
It — and the display was frozen with the
Icon saying — life is good — so I pushed

The button to no avail and took the
Battery out repeatedly which is
Supposed to re-jigger the phone when the
Battery is reinserted and I

Heard a click and saw a point of blue light
Flicker and then a display pronouncing
— Welcome — arose followed by the — life is
Good — revelation — again so I am

Holding the phone against my cheek thinking
I could have used this for warmth in winter.

Can't make a call
can't surf the Internet
no music at the gym
no driving directions no
email no weather info.

It is necessary after buying
A phone to enter a secret password
As a matter of privacy that must
Be entered repeatedly and mine is

Abracadabra1 that I am sure
No one will guess — but it's laborious
To type twice for each application and
My fingertip is blunt and the key is

Tiny and the letter becomes a dot
That can't be read and I fumble and don't
Know whether I typed correctly and I
Get blocked because my identity can

Not be verified repeatedly so
I fight the urge to step upon my phone.

There is a
labyrinthine world
of crypto-technology
of hackers and bots
but I just want music.

Society in America is
Evolving as the old industrial
Infrastructure is being replaced with
The technological innovation

Made possible by computers and the
Internet — and enthusiasts proclaim
Finally people will be free from the
Drudgery of labor but what will the

Truck driver do if he is replaced by
Self-driving vehicles and would it be
Enough to endlessly play video
Games and watch movies on Netflix and post

Messages on Facebook or wouldn't he
Rather find satisfaction by working?

How will people of
average ability
find satisfaction
by playing games
instead of working?

For a change we were meditating in
A cabin in the country and a fly
Was touching our ears with a whine in the
Air — or maybe we were touching the whine

With our ears — over here and over there —
And after our sitting we went outside
With a chainsaw and traffic and music
In the distance and birds nearby and a

River rippling and reflecting and
The clouds transforming and the toppled trees
And leaves decaying in the water and
Infinite detail is impossible

To describe — except that I am touching
And being touched differently than you are.

The compulsion
to be productive
lifted and
consciousness
liberates.

The cottonwood leaves are half-grown outside
My window today and I remember
All the previous years of seeing the
Leaves half-grown and shining in the sunlight

But now I know beyond the sky there are
A hundred billion stars in the Milky
Way and beyond that there are a hundred
Billion galaxies with a hundred

Billions stars in each galaxy and each
Galaxy is expanding rapidly
In the universe and with that context
The reliable seasons of earth seem

Like a separate cottonwood leaf in
The infinity of the cosmos.

Intelligence
curiosity
instability —
I need direction
to channel my energy.

To grasp the meaning of a large number
I need a method of recognition
To furrow my forehead and a million
Seconds amounts to eleven and one

Half days — and a billion seconds amounts
To thirty-one and three quarter years — and
A trillion seconds approaches about
Thirty-two thousand years — and light moves through

The vacuum of space faster than any
Thing at a rate of one hundred eighty-
Six thousand miles per second and the light
From the furthest edge of the universe

Takes about forty-seven billion years to reach
The earth — which is a lengthy afternoon.

A microsecond
is one millionth of one
second — a nanosecond
one billionth and a
picosecond one trillionth.

Imagine a smiling waiter bringing
You a dish of your favorite ice cream
Every second for a trillion seconds —
He will be approaching you while you are

Having coffee with your friends and he will
Be elbowing you while you are driving
To Stillwater and he will be stacking
Dishes while you are taking a shower

And you could not escape him if you were
Giving a speech at a symposium
And if you don't bequeath his services
To your closest relative when you die

He will appear at your resting place for
Thirty-one thousand nine-hundred odd years.

Or you could dispense
with the bother and
receive your allotment
of ice cream in a
trillion picoseconds.

Pointy headed scientists insist the
Universe originated from a
Space no larger than a trillionth of the
Period at the end of this sonnet

And they say in a picosecond the
Cosmos popped into existence in a
Big Bang and was approximately ten
Thousand trillion trillion degrees — which is

Pretty hot — and in a nanosecond
The mass equal to the mass of our own
Milky Way was packed in the space of a
Hydrogen atom — which is pretty dense —

And they say space did not exist until
Popping matter gave itself its texture.

It takes me more
than a nanosecond
to comprehend this
information — more even
than a microsecond.

It is deplorable that a straw was
Discovered in the Marianas Trench
And perhaps to rescue the earth from the
Dispersal of disposable items

It may be helpful where possible to
Turn our implements of convenience
Into fashion accessories and I
Imagine a boutique establishment

Selling remarkable straws with perhaps
Titanium for a military
Gentleman with a tortoise shell case or
Elongated simulated ivory

Or tastefully bejeweled silver or gold
For a status conscious mademoiselle.

We would favor the
planet and engage
ingenuity massage
egocentricity and
boost employment.

Under cherry blossoms on a splendid
Afternoon nothing could make the moment
Better as the blooms take away the strife
I carry and the delicacy of

The petals are captivating and I
Turn to the freshness of growing leaves in
Pioneer Park and the elevated
Bluff allows me to absorb the sweep of

The winding valley and the river and
The sun — in the distance there is the new
Crossing Bridge spanning the river at a
Great height with artistic lines — and the boats

On the water are miniscule but I
Discern a majestic paddle wheeler.

Bees are busy
in the cherry blooms
when weeks ago
the tree was frozen
the branches were bare.

The scent of apple blossoms and lilacs
And the reappearance of cherry blooms
After a prolonged and dreary winter
On the occasion of a sunny day

When the leaves are almost grown and the air
Is mild again are a resurrection
Of beauty and joy that remind me of
Light-hearted childhood and easy going

Faith that everything is OK — and there
Is a touch of sadness in knowing that the
Blossoms will scatter and the perfume will
Dissipate in a few hours but the

Sun will be prominent for many months
And we will have thunderstorms and lightning.

There is
nothing crabby
about luscious
crabapple
blossoms.

On the occasion of apple blossoms
I celebrate the flowering and the
Dissipation as the blooms delight me
With their delicacy and beauty as

They reappear when the leaves are almost
Fully grown and the sun is extending
Energy and the earth is reviving
And the grass is growing in a shower

Of light and the sky is brilliant again
And I wonder why I am moved by the
Brief blossoming of a flowering tree
Separate from the events of my life and

When the petals are dispersing onto
The asphalt of the driveway I am sad.

Why is the
appearance and
disappearance
so delicately
beautiful?

Women in cyberspace are out of touch
Which doesn't mean they have no influence
And I have dabbled on dating sites and
Fashioned a profile with photographs but

My enthusiasm is haphazard
Because there is a miniscule range of
Compatibility because I want
Someone luscious and lascivious and

They want someone with bags of money and
I am a wordy intellectual
Who is a visionary mystic — but
I am wearily insouciant too

And I can't summon the energy to
Pick up the phone and compose a message.

Somewhere
Cleopatra is
waiting but I
can't summon
intensity.

After waking I was sore below my
Belly and found a bulging red welt that
Wasn't there yesterday so I ransacked
My memory and remembered the strange

Sensation when lifting the one hundred
Pound dumbbell forty times in a row and
The unusual pain didn't slow me
But I am sphere of consciousness and

From the periphery events waylay
Me — and the doctor said that I ruptured
My abdominal wall by tearing a
A muscle and am rewarded with a

Hematoma that makes wearing pants and
Walking a delectable affliction.

He said I am
not young anymore
and it isn't a
hernia so really
I am lucky.

The river is rippling again and
The river is sparkling with light and
The river is also glassy and I
Am imagining the spinning of the

Earth and electro-magnetic waves and
Gravitational waves rippling in
The atmosphere and interstellar space
And I am absorbing waves of photons

And sub-atomic particles and am
Awash in micro and radio waves
And the earth is rolling about the sun
Compelled by sloping space and space is not
Empty but is undulating about

Me as if I were a prominent rock
Being polished by a musical creek.

Waves of light
are bouncing off the
white and purple lilacs
and cresting away
into my eyes.

I am ambulatory but mostly
Sitting because of the hematoma
Near my pelvis and when it burst in the
Night as I was tossing and sleeping I

Didn't notice until I gingerly
Pulled the elastic band of my shorts and
Saw the open wound and the smeared blood that
Stuck to hair and I ignored the tearing

Sensation because I am a tough guy
And I shaved around the area and
Cleaned the wound and applied a bandage that
Needed to be securely taped in place

And now I have to sit on my ass and
Wait because I can't be exercising.

I was a little
too enthusiastic
with a dumbbell and
won't do that particular
exercise again.

Atoms combine to form molecules and
There are as many molecules in my
Eye as stars in the Milky Way and the
Air I breathe and the water I drink are

The same molecules that living beings
Have breathed and drunk as long as beings have
Lived on the earth — and the hidden structure
Of the cosmos is identified by

The persistence of scientists while on
My own I operate in a narrow
Range of perception believing myself
The center of the universe — even

When I comprehend the fact that I am
A temporary sphere of consciousness.

Apple blossoms and
lilacs effuse a scent
wafting in waves of
molecules penetrating
me with happiness.

As I was lying in bed before dawn
There was the rain and the thunder through the
Window and I heard the curvature of
The earth rebounding in the thunder or

I thought so and then it was time to feed
The cats and change water in the water
Dishes and brush the cats and make coffee
And attend to the litter box and have

Breakfast and by the time the shaving and
Showering was done and I was sitting
Meditating on the zafu and the
Zabuton there was light and birdsong through

The window and I heard the various
Songs of the birds that words cannot capture.

It is easier to
to detach from disruptive
emotions when I
practice letting them go and
drink in the sights and the sounds.

I knew Clark as a red headed rascal
From New York City who was my roommate
In a half-way house and afterwards in
A rented house on Grand Avenue in

St. Paul when we were attempting to be
Free of alcohol and drug addiction
By going to meetings and practicing
A program more than thirty years ago

And his mother is a famous singer
Living a life of exclusionary
Celebrity and I knew Clark to be
Curious and adventurous and strict

With sobriety but he encountered
Some difficulty and ended his life.

At a gathering
of three thousand sober people
I was surprised to
be touched by memory as
his mother told their story.

Every addict trying to be sober
Has to surrender justifications
Because self-pity and resentments are
Poisonous and it is not helpful to

Dwell on unfairness when dwelling on the
Unfairness precludes optimism and
Strengthens the emotions of defeat — and
The balancing of thoughts and emotions

Goes on continuously in subtle
Degrees and if the addict neglects to
Communicate with fellow addicts and
Share in a strength of community that

Is founded on intangible power
He forgets that addiction is deadly.

Clark broke off
communication
and was lost inside
a labyrinth of
misery.

The monarch butterflies born in August
In North America will migrate the
Thousands of miles to California
Or Mexico and they leave in fall and

Return in spring and somehow may return
To the same tree — the three generations
Of monarchs that are born from the spring to
The end of July aren't hardy enough to

Fly the distance and they frolic in the
Air for only a few weeks before they
Die — but every monarch butterfly starts
As an egg becomes a caterpillar

Weaves a chrysalis about itself and
Epitomizes metamorphosis.

The fluttering
monarch butterfly
is delicately beautiful
and poisonously
unappetizing.

Maybe the monarch butterfly uses
The foothills of the Rocky Mountains as
A guide and in its course it traverses
Brooks and rapids and broad flowing rivers

And maybe on its journey it takes a
Break by the Colorado River
In the Grand Canyon — and afterwards it
Flickers up the cliffs and out again — and

When the wind blows and the rain is pelting
It would have to take shelter but it is
Hard to imagine such a delicate
Creature continuously fluttering

As if its motion and direction were
A destiny and a satisfaction.

The butterfly beats
the air with its wings
and by force of will
and leverage it stays
aloft and flying.

Just thinking about possibilities
Makes me excited because I could meet
Anyone on Facebook when I set up
A page and post an introductory

Message with the photo of me at the
Gym on the mat sitting in the lotus
Position as if I were doing Zen
While wearing my sleeveless exercise gear

Showing the Buddha and lotus tattoos
On my shoulders that will communicate
So much about me beyond what words can
Do and maybe I will become friends with

People in Germany and Katmandu
Or I could engage a celebrity.

Of course I could be
chatting with a vivacious
and dimpled blonde
who in reality is
an obese guy in Pittsburg.

It is a couple of vertical posts
And a couple of horizontal tops
That the Japanese call a tori gate
And they usually paint it vermillion —

The name tori means the abode of birds
And the gate has no purpose except to
Signify the crossing of the mundane
To the sacred and I like the simple

Symbol and wonder how many times a
Day I could exit the ordinary
And encounter the ethereal if
I were not in a rush to get things done —

Sometimes in a frenzy and sometimes in
A quiet moment I am bedazzled.

Little by little
or all at once
I see beauty
And vastness.

I can see the weight of a cottonwood
Puff floating in the air and the air that
I breathe is made visible when the puffs
Are floating — and the smaller ones will rise

And meander but the heaviest will
Drop consistently and I can follow the
Journey of one or I can consider
The multitude that reminds me of

The people on a congested street with
Each person on a mission while the whole
Is a spectacle of seeming chaos —
And then the puffs are caught up in a breeze

And the curving current is visible
In the sinuous flowing of the puffs.

The cottonwood leaves
are fully grown and
pristine — and the sun
is touching the green leaves
over layering yellow.

I am a child who desires the moon
Seeing its untouchable allure and
Watching its transformation from a sphere
To a crescent noticing its presence

Even in the morning and afternoon
Appearing in a blue sky surpassing
The clouds as a jewel always beyond my
Grasping as an otherworldly something

Though the moon doesn't have the drama of
A sunrise or the power to change the
Seasons and determine life and I know
It's just a rock without an atmosphere —

The moon is in my heart as a symbol
Of beauty outshining explanation.

The moon is just a
mirror of the sun
prominent in the
night and elusive
during the day.

Kit Cat wakes earlier than I do and
He is smarter than I prefer and he
Did something this morning for the first time —
He used the door to my bedroom as a

Drum to wake me up — and it sounded as
If he rose on his hind legs and hammered
On the door with all his weight with his front
Paws and he is weighty and sinuous —

And for a reason I don't understand
He wanted inside my room even though
There was an open window to look out
And listen out in the dining room — and

He just would not stop — and I thought if I
Surrender he will do this everyday.

Curiosity
and stupidity
got the better of
me — proving I am
a pushover.

Someday I would love to vacation in
The Bahamas or the Rocky Mountains
For an exotic experience but
Today I am at home in Stillwater —

And now spring is transitioning into
Summer without hindrance and all I have
To do is be attentive — and I am
Listening to the wind tossing the leaves

Throughout the morning the afternoon and
The evening and I am allowing
The persistence of the wind in the leaves
To fill me with unexplainable peace

And joy — and I don't need explanations —
The wind in the leaves is ethereal.

The trees tossing
in the wind are making
the breathe of life
audible and
visible.

The blue sky is exceptional and the
Earth appears blue from the vantage of the
Moon and there is not another planet
With breathable blue air in the cosmos

We are aware of and we are searching
The fourteen billion light years of space and
Set among the brilliance of stars planets
Are almost impossible to find so

Given the impersonal and immense
Nature of reality there is no
Reason why the sound of the wind in the
Leaves should be so reassuring but then

In spring with the reappearance of leaves
There is the resurrection of sighing.

In the wind
in the trees the
breath of life
is audible
is visible.

Rain drumming on the roof and flowing in
The metal downspouts with the cool moist air
Reminds me that this morning is forming
A new manifestation — as I am

Moving about the house feeding the cats
Emptying the dehumidifier
Washing the dishes while all the windows
Are open and I am wearing a warm

Shirt listening to the consistency
Of rain speculating — who will be there
This morning and what stories will there be —
And I like unpredictability

Balanced with a reliable routine
Forming this immaculate morning.

Rain drumming on
the car — going
to meet friends.

It is helpful to set aside some time
After feeding the cats in the morning
To cross my legs and straighten my back and
Circle my hands with the tips of my thumbs

Touching — and while my body is poised and
Relaxed my mind discloses itself to
Me and there may be conversation from
A phone call or music from yesterday

Or maybe an old pattern will assert
Itself rehearsing an aggravation
That may be mixed with satisfaction and
Sometimes I imagine thoughts arising

From the circle within my fingers as
The tips of my thumbs are barely touching.

I hold my thoughts
gently within my
fingers and palms
and my thumbs are
poised touching.

I need to be gentle with myself when
There are no easy solutions and my
Mind returns to comparisons and
Justifications and the unfairness

Of circumstances because I am not
The only person who feels gloomy on
Occasion — and I need to recognize
That sometimes my intellect becomes a

Labyrinth of contradicting puzzles
With my thoughts churning uselessly — because
That is what my thoughts and emotions do
Sometimes when I assume a point of view —

When I don't know what to do with myself
I have to believe I am loveable.

I am
exquisitely
situated to
discover what
love is.

Once a month I leave my Zen Bridge group of
Meditators after meditation
And do without the conversation at
The coffee shop and go to a meeting

Of Washington County Republicans
For conversation at a family
Owned restaurant and though the differences of
The groups are not as tribal as between

The Irish Catholics and the Protestants
I do approximate being a spy
In suspicious camps and touch the edges
Of the sharp attitudes on either side —

Sharing a mission and urgency is
Intoxicating — letting be is hard.

There is enough
deluded honesty
to keep everyone
enthusiastic
and arguing.

As a consumer of the news and a
Composer of essays I reinforce
My compendium of data points and
Marshall my facts in order but unlike

My colleagues I don't go to bed and wake
Up angry and I'm not surrounded by
Politicos and activists burning
With the latest outrage and if I were

Whom could I trust? Every morning my cats
Are awake before me and they express
Uniqueness without sophistication
And this morning there is a steady breeze

And the leaves are tossing and creating
The most peaceful and satisfying sound.

The simple fact
of breathing and
beginning the day with
optimism is
unsurpassable.

My chin is on the heel of my hand and
My elbow is placed upon a board that
Serves as a desktop for a keyboard and
A computer — and I am quite confused —

Because it seems the computer the board
And me — and the cottonwood outside the
Window — are each composed of atoms with
Nuclei around which electrons are

Swirling — and it seems that most of the space
That encloses atoms is empty and
So everything about me consists of
Essentially empty space and yet I

Recall the morning a pileated
Woodpecker was pecking the cottonwood.

Are the words that
arise from the
molecules
of my brain
empty?

Somehow scientists identify the
Nature of particles much too small to
See by using logical deduction
By employing precise instruments like

The Large Hadron Collider that is a
Twenty-seven kilometer ring of
Superconducting magnets that directs
Streams of particles accelerated as

Fast as possible into collision
Exposing gluons and bosons and quarks
And leaping leptons and matter anti-
Matter annihilation revealing

If God created the earth in seven
Days God is capable of precision.

Beyond our
technology
there is only
mathematical
postulation.

It's amazing a mathematician
Can compose an equation describing
The curving space of a hillside in terms
Of mass and energy — and amazing

Scientists also dissect the cosmos
Into relative speeds and distances —
And it is a little confounding that
An unrelenting application of

Logic and deduction exposes the
Terrifying impersonality
Of the immense and the minute without
Providing a basis for compassion

Or for a very useful description
Of being alive and learning to love.

Once I became
a father I don't
believe there's
ever an end to
being a Dad.

Walking underneath the rain I am more
Receptive than I know when a single
Drop impacts upon my forehead — but not
Until I saw the size of the spot of

Wetness on the concrete and I passed a
Puddle and noticed the splash and ripple
Was I fully aware these were very
Big raindrops falling from the clouds — and I

Recalled a moment ago the instant
Of being struck the size of the plop was
Apparent but I would not have noticed
Without the reinforcing evidence

Everywhere before me — proving I am
A vessel of transient sensations.

Rain is falling
in waves of
intensity and
they are slanting
in cool gusts of wind.

Dear reader if you are reading me now
You have probably read other poems
Also and I would like to thank you for
Your interest and your time and by the way

I am not gay but wordy and geeky
And like to figure things out and now you
Are the object of rumination — and
Because you are reading poetry and

Not obsessing on Facebook or Twitter
You are likely to be independent
And intelligent and I wouldn't guess
You're a man because men drive pickup trucks

And mess with tools in the garage so please
Know I am single and available.

You can always
reach me at
info@bumble.com.

Alligators and an impending sense
Of doom were the vestiges of a dream
That dissipated once Johnnie began
To incessantly yowl for his cat food

And I tried to remember the entire
Milieu of this episode of terror
But the details had slipped through my fingers
So to speak as I was opening the

Cans of food and separating the three
Cats into their isolated rooms and
All I could do was to ponder the world
Of physics and the scientist who wrote

The book I was reading last night who wants
Evidence of something deeper than quarks.

How can we
verify
measure
quantify
dreams?

It is there every morning in the tank
The surviving one of the four that lived
For twenty years and I remember my
Dad would drop the flakes of food and watch as

Silver dollars would flit so speedily
Around the water snatching the dropping
Flakes but my father died years ago and
I was not enthusiastic about

Maintaining the aquarium but I
Have a routine of changing the water
And cleaning the filter and feeding the
Fish and this one is more interesting —

He is about the size of a silver
Dollar with roving intelligent eyes.

He watches me
everyday and now
I am watching
him.

Jennifer is in my circle of friends
And she is the captain of a rolling
Rectangle that contains children on the
Way to and from a school and she enjoys

Driving the bus and she loves marshalling
The students and would like to continue
Everyday and Harold is a retired
Marine who also drives a school bus but

He comes to our circle with horrible
Tales of the devious behavior and
The disrespect he is attempting to
Endure — and maybe the assortment of

Kids is different or perhaps the
Permutations of the divers are key.

Over all there
could be a
balancing out of
repulsion and
attraction.

It's a dark morning with the watery
Sound of rain continuously coming
Through the windows and I have a choice of
Wearing long pants or shorts — and I'm not

Meeting anyone so there is no need
Of formality — and even though the air
Is chilly now it is most likely to
Be hot and muggy by this afternoon

So I will wear my shorts and my clogs too
Because I believe not wearing socks is
The epitome of liberation —
I was given the clogs and they are too

Big but I do like them — and now I will
Stay warm by wearing a long sleeve sweatshirt.

Sitting at my desk
I only have to
tilt my feet down
and suddenly
I am barefoot.

After the cats have been separated
And fed and then brushed they can do as they
Wish while I have to change the water in
Their dishes and attend to the litter

Boxes and the box upstairs is sticky
Because of the gooey medicine that
Henry needs for his kidney disease and
Then I can do as I want and coffee

Is a priority and this morning
While I read my daily meditation
Books on the periphery Kit Cat leaps
Through the air from the bed and he lands

With a thud on the floor and he thunders
After Johnnie into the dining room.

Henry likes to be
brushed and as I
sit on the floor he
nudges my calf with
the top of his head.

The solstice is approaching again with the
Counterbalancing of the longest day
And the shortest night and afterwards the
The nights will begin to lengthen until

A balancing with the shortest day in
December — while in Minnesota this
Morning it is chilly and damp and the
Ants are busy in a humongous hill

In my yard and the grass does need cutting
This afternoon and the temperature
Was ninety degrees a few days ago
But now a chill is returning in the

Morning — proving that we are never far
From February in Minnesota.

The border of my
yard along the street near
the corner of the
driveway shows the damage of
a reckless city snowplow.

Gravity and dark matter are drawing
The Andromeda and the Milky Way
Galaxies together and within four
Billion years the hundred billion stars of

The Milky Way will mix with the trillion
Stars of Andromeda as the black holes
At the centers of the galaxies will
Circulate and eventually will

Combine into one extraordinary
Black hole whirling all the stars in a new
Array and whether a passing star will
Strip the earth from our sun and into its

Orbit or fling us into empty space
Or whether we will be OK — who knows?

It is hard to tell
from my comfy office
chair that we are caught
in the spiraling of
the Milky Way.

We each have an individualized
Expiration date when our lives will end
And the earth is also not exempt from
A fiery death when the sun burns up

Its hydrogen and commences to fuse
Helium nuclei into carbon
And then the sun will swell hundreds of times
Bigger than now and the sun will swallow

The planets Mercury and Venus and
The sun will loom larger and larger and
The oceans will evaporate and the
Lands will be molten and there will be an

End of solstices equinoxes and
Lunar eclipses before the earth burns.

The sun will not be
a red giant in
an afternoon but
in five billion years
of afternoons.

From the vantage of today the Pueblo
People who lived in the hollows of the
Cliffs who built adobe homes and worshiped
The sun seem simple and innocent as

The sun was determinate of so much —
Drenching lifetimes with light — and imagine
The contrasting of the day with the night
With stars and the comfort of a small fire —

And perhaps they shared our frailties and
Were as prone to anger and fear as we
Are and they needed to ascribe meaning
To what happened by considering the

Constellations and by retelling the
Mythical stories about courage.

Even with our
knowledge of the
cosmos have we
outgrown needing
stories about courage?

A black hole that can whirl a trillion stars
About itself is not something that can
Be safely ignored and where do the stars
Go that disappear into the hole — and

It is said that vanished stars are compiled
On themselves to a point of infinite
Density inside the hole and said that
Millions of light years is not far enough

To escape the vortex of the hole and
It is speculated even space/time
Collapses inside the hole and time is
Instantaneous and so a word is

Used to describe the inconceivable —
The black hole is a singularity.

The hole where things
go to vanish is an
organizing factor
creating motion
and direction.

Imagine galaxies are vanishing
Beyond the horizon of telescopes —
Cosmic energy is dissipating —
The temperature is plummeting to

Absolute zero — the trillions of stars
Of the galaxies are flickering out —
The massive black hole of our galaxy
Is evaporating — imagine the

Dark mass and dark energy dissolving —
The universe is in a dark era
With molecules disintegrating — with
Particles diffusing and drifting and

At this curious time of day it would
Be difficult to make a ham sandwich.

I would be on the
corner checking the
weather app on my phone
waiting impatiently
for the next Big Bang.

Waiting and Loving

The attraction is understandable —
He speaks of hardship and aggression and
The advantages of retribution
That compelled the respect he exacted

And he told me that her mother believes
She is bad and never will be any
Good and that her ex-husband is using
Their daughter to sell heroin and that

Every member of her family would
Rather she remain an addict and a
Drunk but that she is doing her best to
Be sober and there is something about

Her that he loves beyond sympathy and
She is the only woman he wants.

There comes a wounding
that makes living differently
imperative and
he needs inexhaustible
power greater than himself.

It is nonsense to be asked to do a
Moral inventory on yourself when
You love an alcoholic and cannot
Stop loving her when she encourages

You and makes a show of caring about
You and sets the table for an evening
Of enjoyment but she disappoints and
Even seems to be purposely hurtful

And you are angry and confused and yet
Cannot stop loving her no matter what —
Sometimes doing what is necessary
Doesn't make sense within the chaos of

Alcoholism when everything you do
For her doesn't make any difference.

Didn't cause it
can't control it
and cannot cure it —
so why are you doing
what you are doing?

I admire a love hardy enough to
Endure the neglect coincident with
Addiction as the addict is rising
From deep waters and is struggling and

Needs to break to the surface and breathe the
Life giving air — and the addict is not
Capable of keeping promises or
Of making trustworthy choices or of

The giving and taking of love — because
Learning to love is difficult without
Experience — and I admire the
Willingness to wait for sobriety

But there is no guarantee that she can
Rise to the surface and emerge safely.

He loves the flair she
has in choosing clothes and when
they talk the night goes
by in an instant and
songs remind him of her.

The attraction is understandable
Because his mother practiced punishing
Him without motherly love and he learned
To harden his emotions as a child

And how is loved learned without a mother's
Original love? The woman he loves shared
The same privations and neglect and
They share the same suspicious attitude

And they did not escape the company
Of predators for many years but he
Sees specialness in her elevating
Her above the other women he knew

And this feeling of love arose and he
Was unprepared and disoriented.

He discovered love
makes the waiting
possible even
without a surety
of return.

He inherited from his mother a
Determination to seize what he wants
And he used his intelligence to see
The vulnerabilities in people

And he learned to apply leverage to
Bend people to his will and he was
Good at persuasion and he was better
At intimidation because he knew

Recklessness is terrifying but he
Also knows that fighting for the scraps he
Thought he needed among people who were
Just like him — even if he were stronger —

Brought him no satisfaction and there is
A hole in his soul he cannot ignore.

He knows he didn't
know how to live and
inescapable
meanness is
dispiriting.

He has absorbed the impact of car and
Motorcycle accidents and he feels
The left-over pain today and he was
As reckless as any addict could be

But he is not alcoholic and can
Stop drinking and drugging when he wants to
But living without satisfaction and
Loving a woman who is an addict

Brought the gift of desperation and drove
Him into the rooms of recovery
Because there was nowhere else to go and
He was willing to do anything to

Alleviate the perplexity and
The frustration and the futility.

When he held her hand
the connection was
different from any
other woman and she
sang and read to him.

She was not ready for marriage she said
And he waited a year and within the
Year she relapsed and in the summer there
Was rejoicing and in the autumn there

Was hesitation and he is waiting
Another year without conversation
With her but the songs he hears in stores and
The words he reads in books remind him of

Her and in the meantime he is learning
How to be respectful and kind with the
People he knows and he is opening
His heart for spiritual solutions and

He is abiding time with patience and
Growing roots into his higher power.

He's taking time to
listen to friends and to help
his father repair
a truck and renovate the
property and land for sale.

They call the building they converted from
A cattle shelter a shop and that is
Where he is in his free time with his Dad
Amongst mechanical equipment and

His Dad is divorcing a second wife
And Dad is a retired overland truck
Driver and Dad remains as stubborn as
Ever but is weaker and when working

With machinery Dad is easily
Confused and needs the knowledge and the skills
Of the son who can do in minutes what
Would have taken hours or would not have been

Done and if the son were not cooking the
Father would not be eating much at all.

When the son was young
the father thought it right that
the son struggle without
help because that is
what grandfather did.

His Dad is selling the house and the farm
And has been talking about going south
Away from the cold winters but Dad has
No definite place to go and Dad is

Always finding new repairs for the truck
And there's a futility about the
Talk as if Dad outlived expectations
And doesn't want to look beyond the next

Modification of the truck and the
Endless fiddling with mechanical
Things is all Dad can do and the son is
Taking the responsibility and

Seeing that Dad is eating and doing
What he can to make Dad comfortable.

The son talks about
moving to Colorado
but the question of
what to do with the woman
he loves is unresolved.

The mariners used sails to catch the wind
And sometimes they suffered under the sun
When there was no wind to move them — and God
Divided the Red Sea and rescued the

People from Pharaoh and He gave Moses
The Ten Commandments and the burden of
Leading the people in the desert for
Forty years — and the mariners didn't

Abandon the seas because they suffered —
And Moses didn't lead his people back
To Egypt because it was difficult —
Burdens are made lighter by sharing them

But the burden is heavy for leaders
Who find their courage when necessary.

Faith means doing the
best possible with
confusion and believing
something good
will happen.

Once there is a touch
of transformation
the mean old ways are
no longer appealing and
we wait for good direction.

— *Tekkan*

www.ingramcontent.com/pod-product-compliance
Lightning Source LLC
Chambersburg PA
CBHW052104070526
44584CB00017B/2326